What Is It?

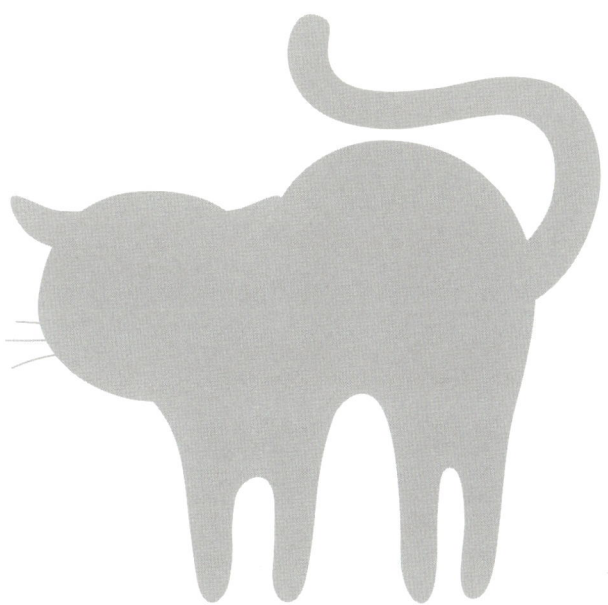

Seed
Learning

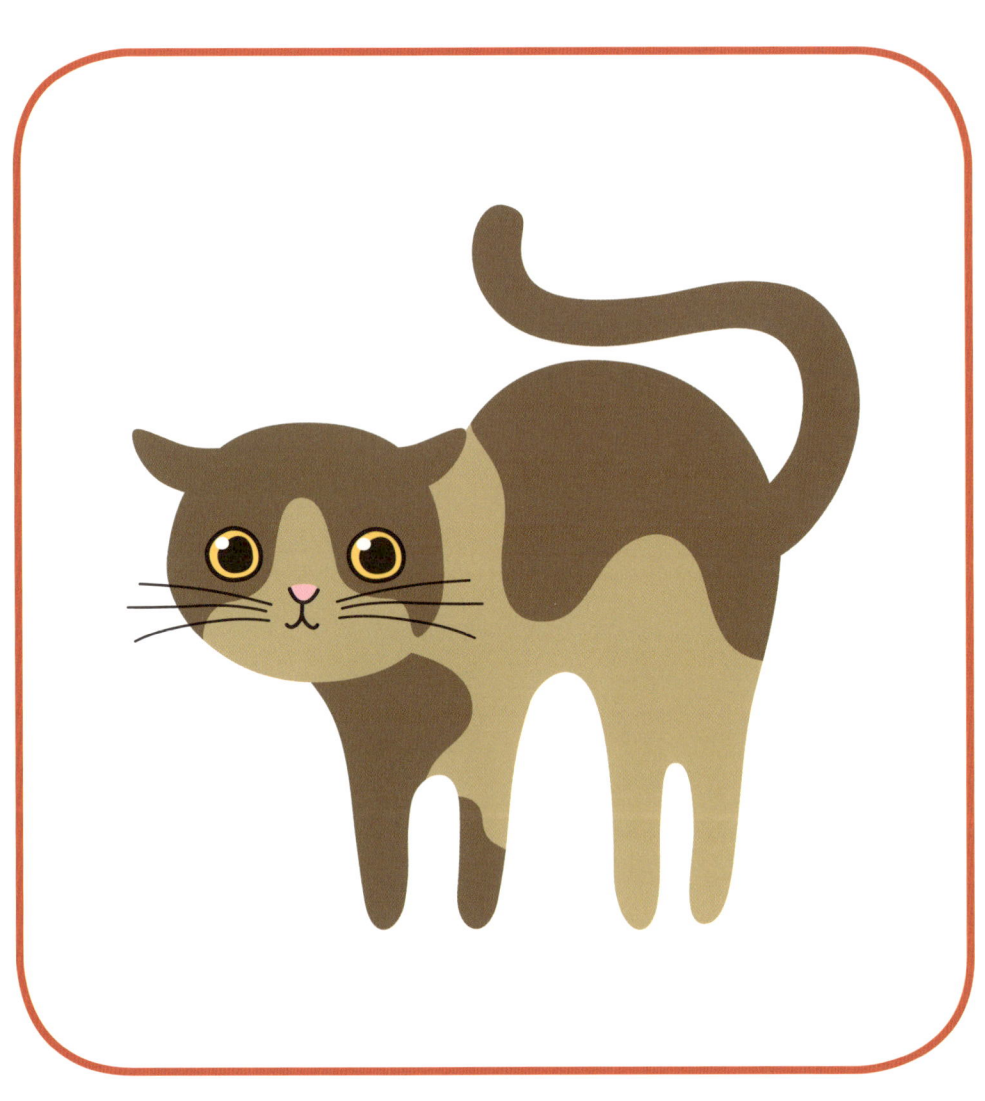

cat

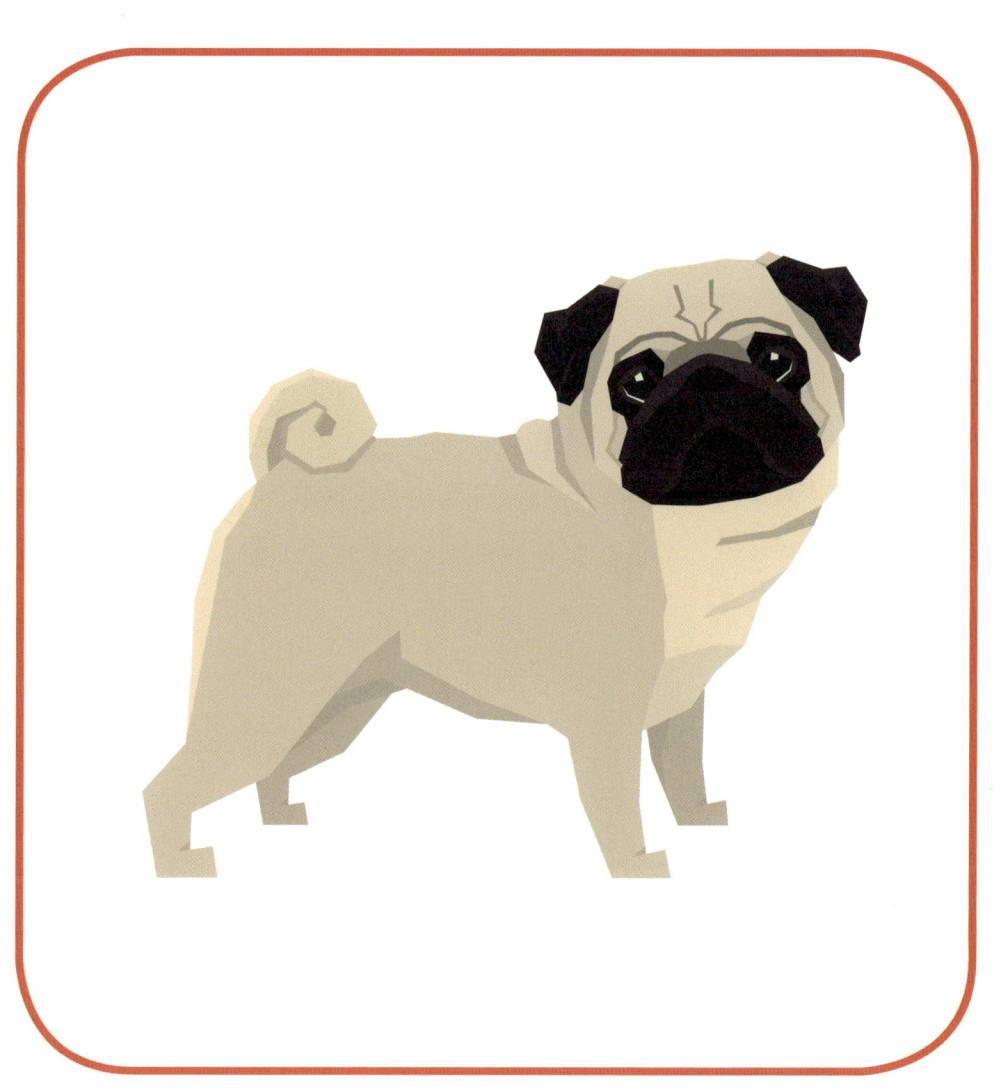

dog

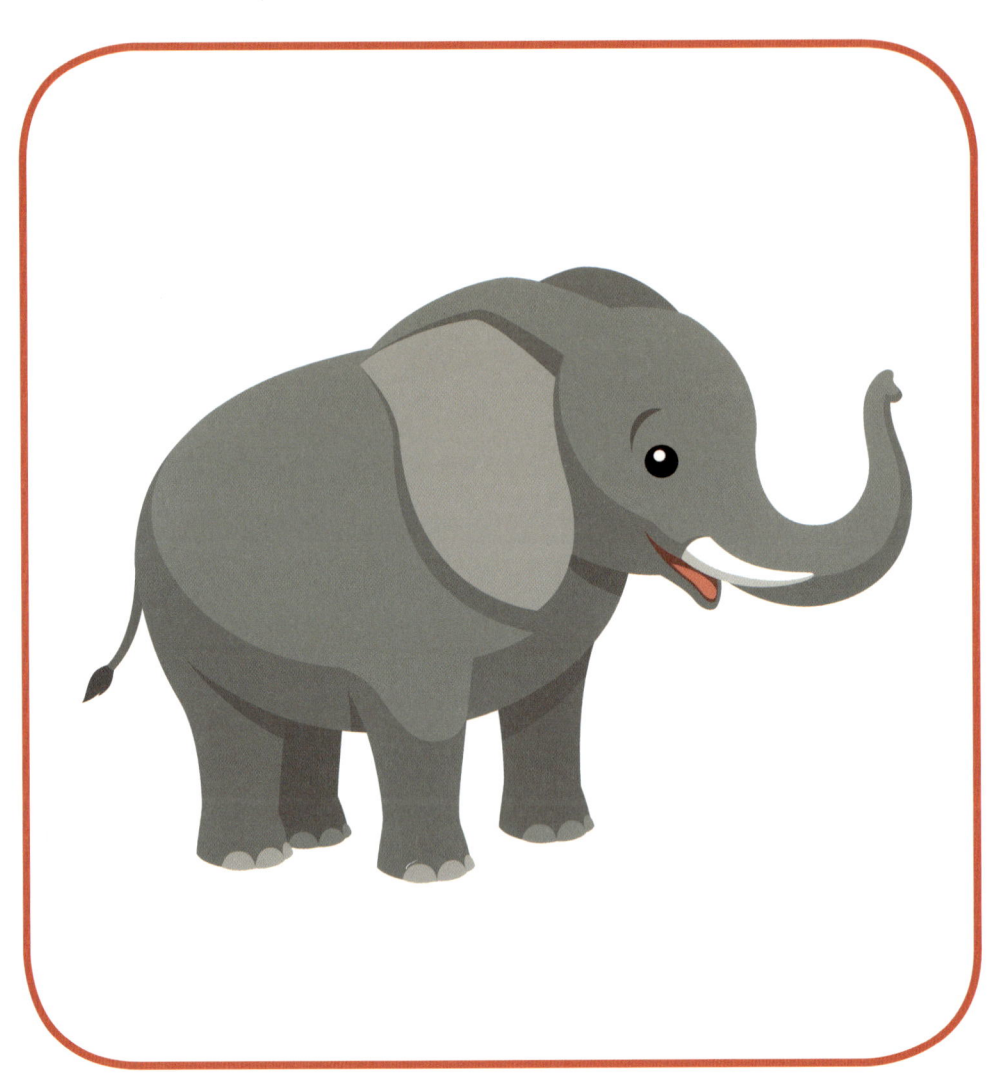

elephant

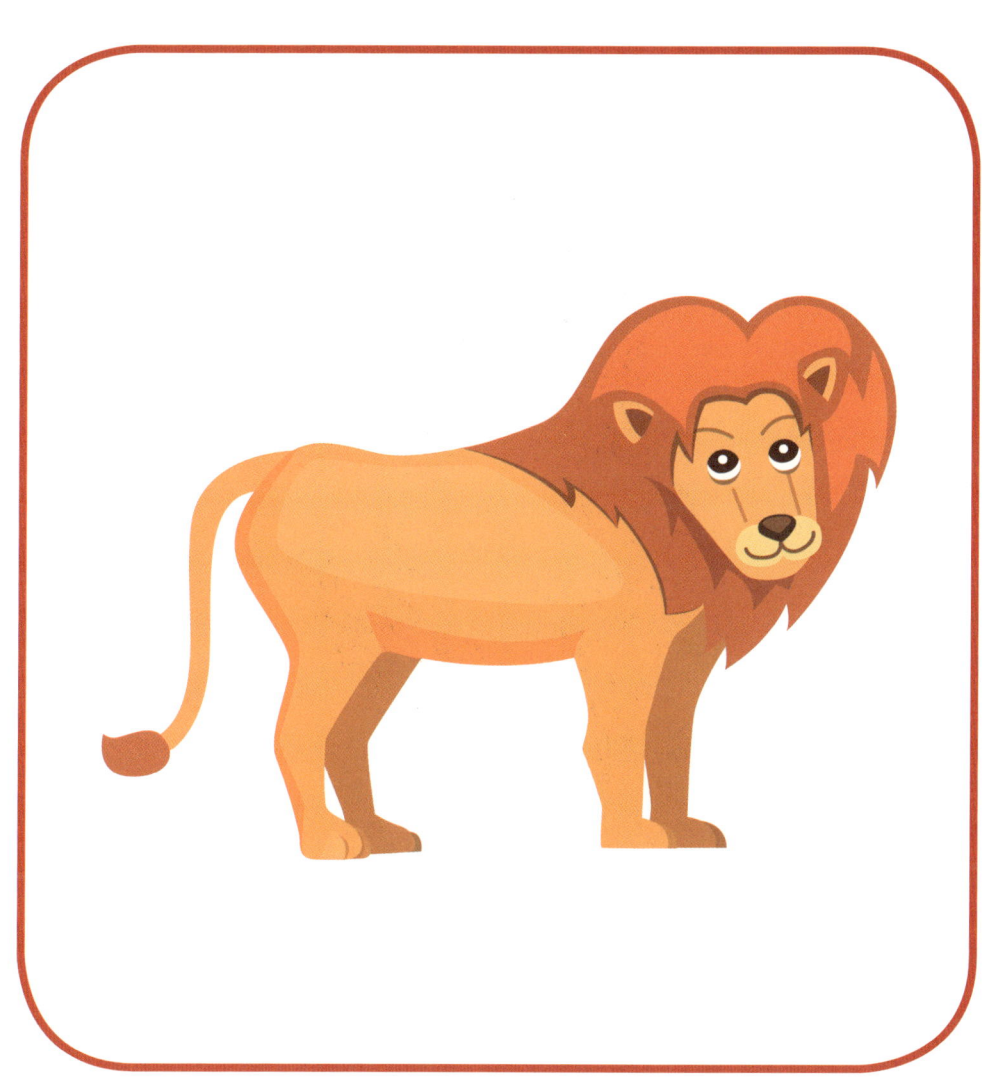

lion

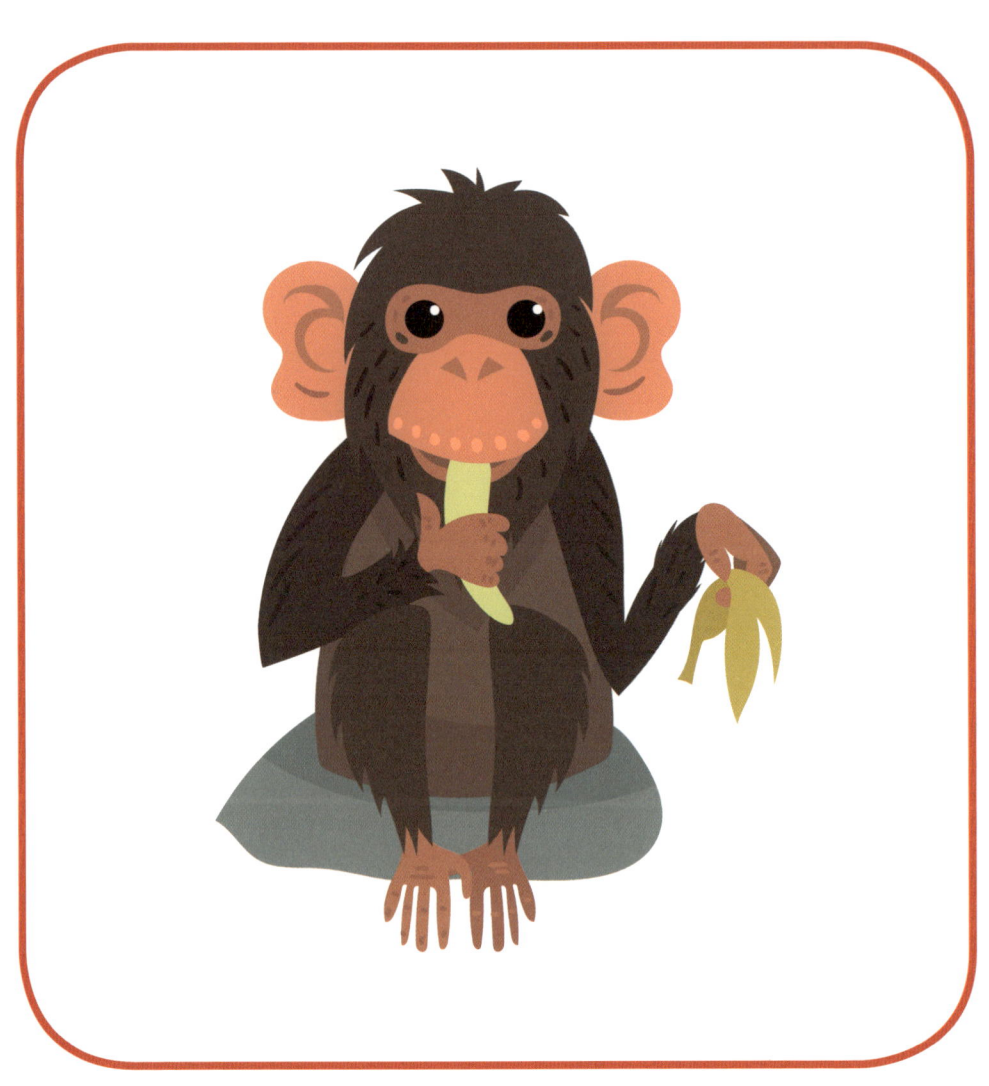

monkey

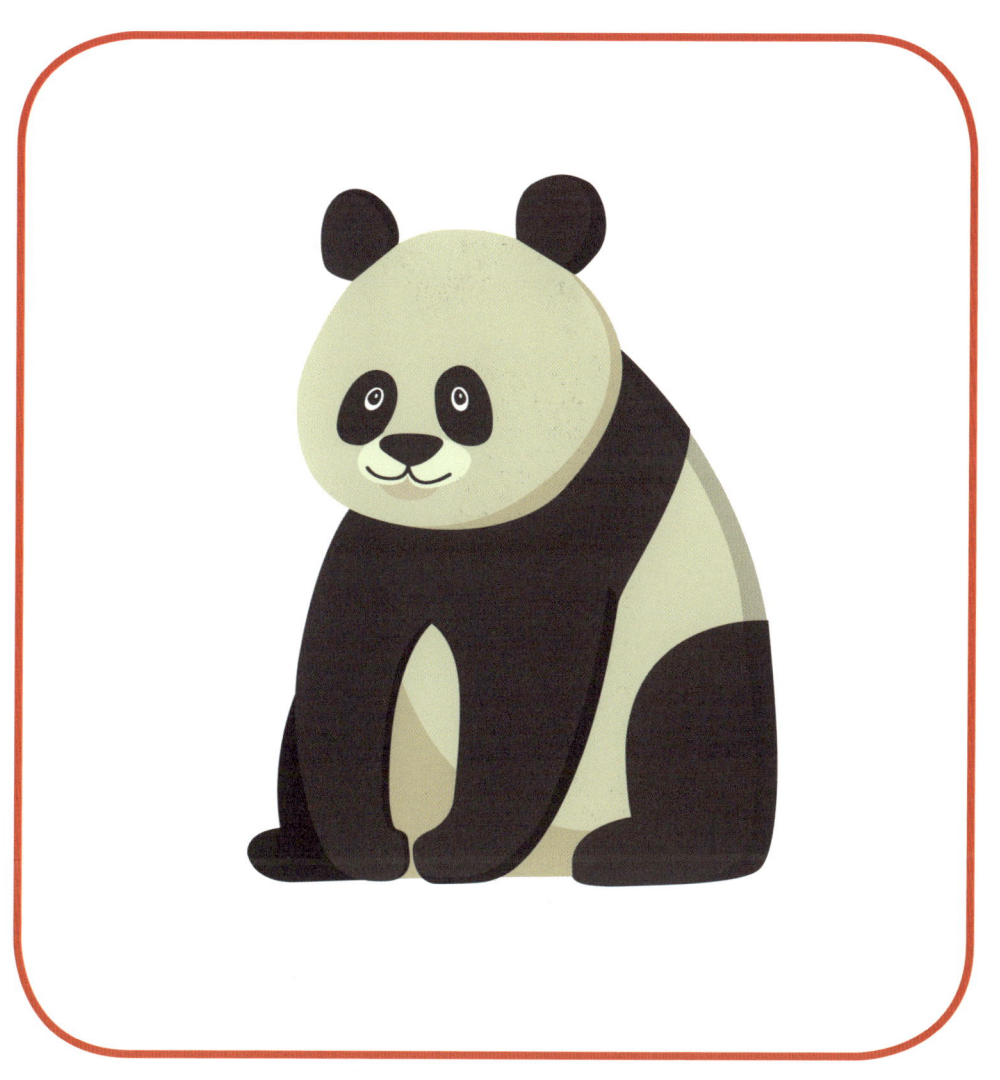

panda

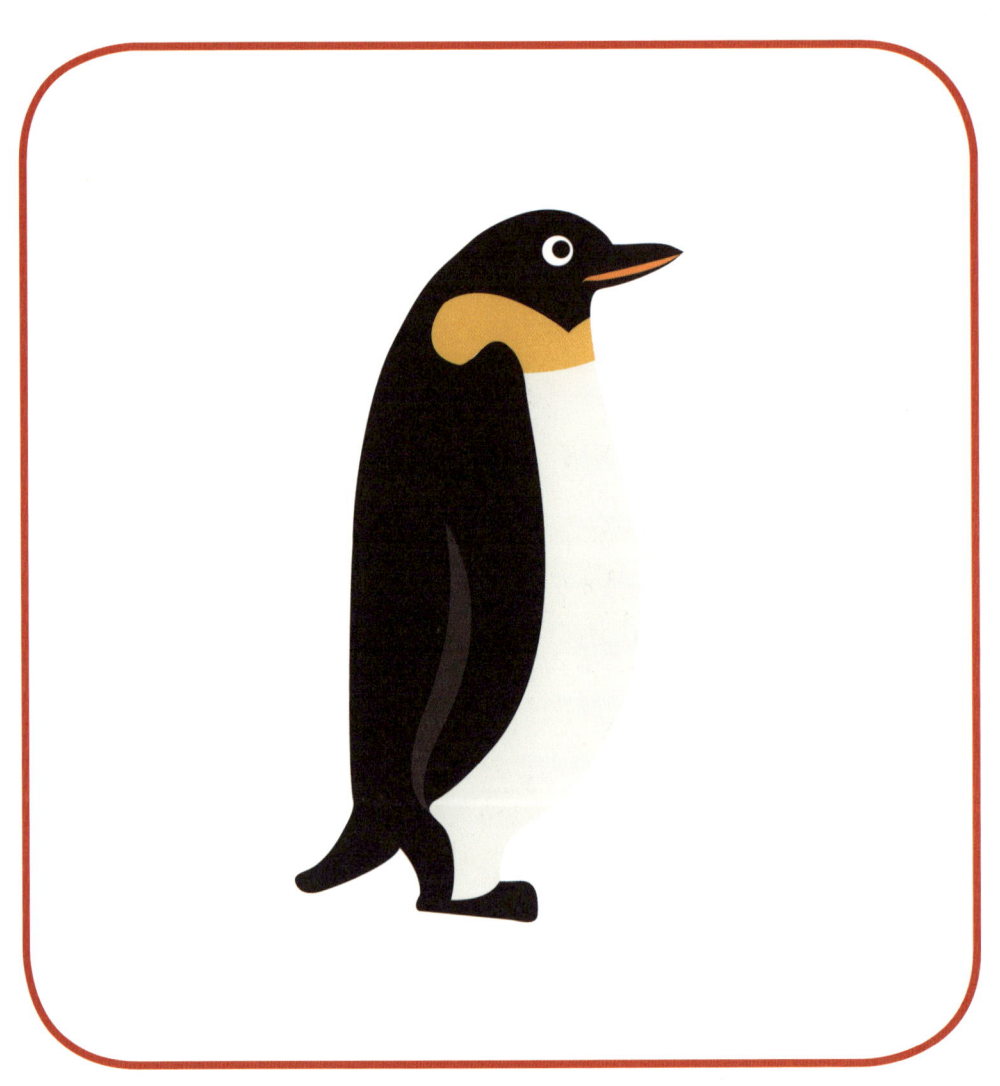

penguin

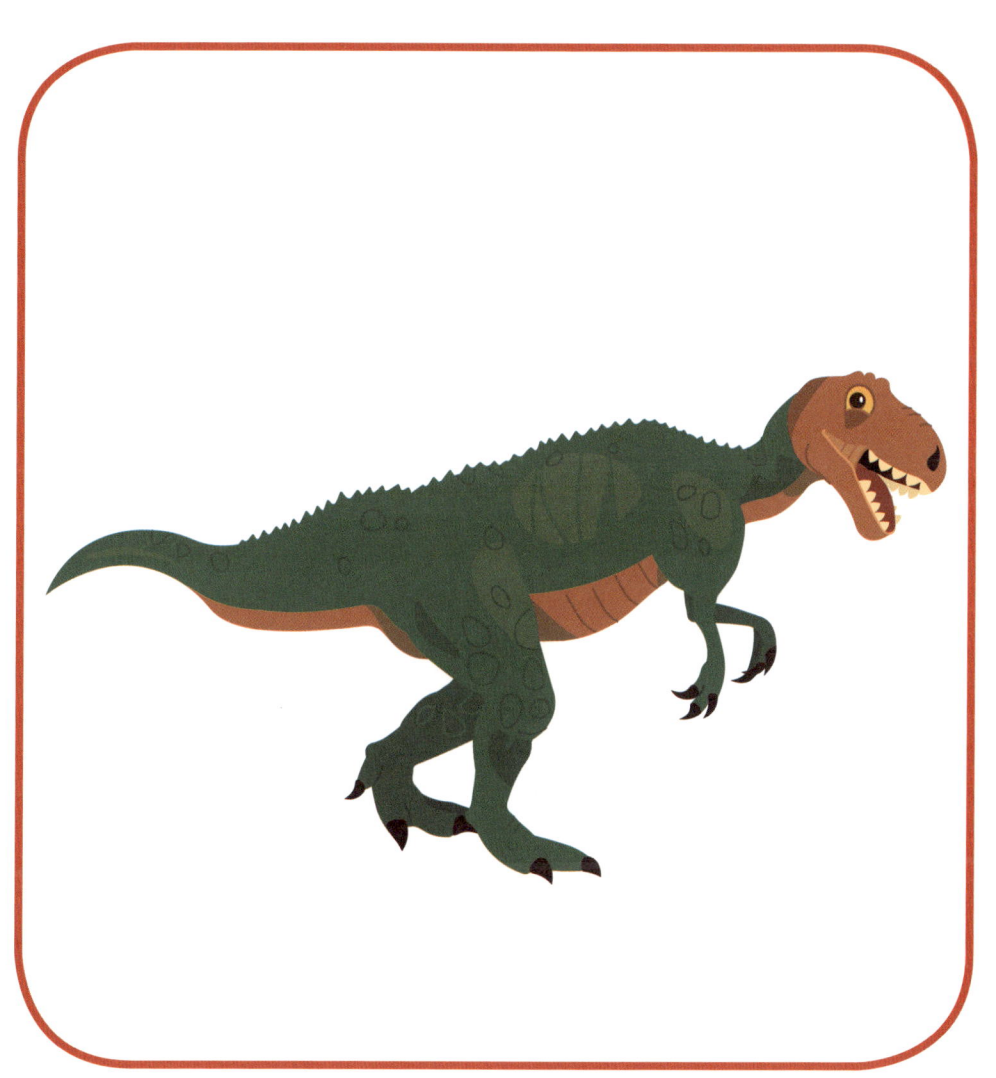

dinosaur

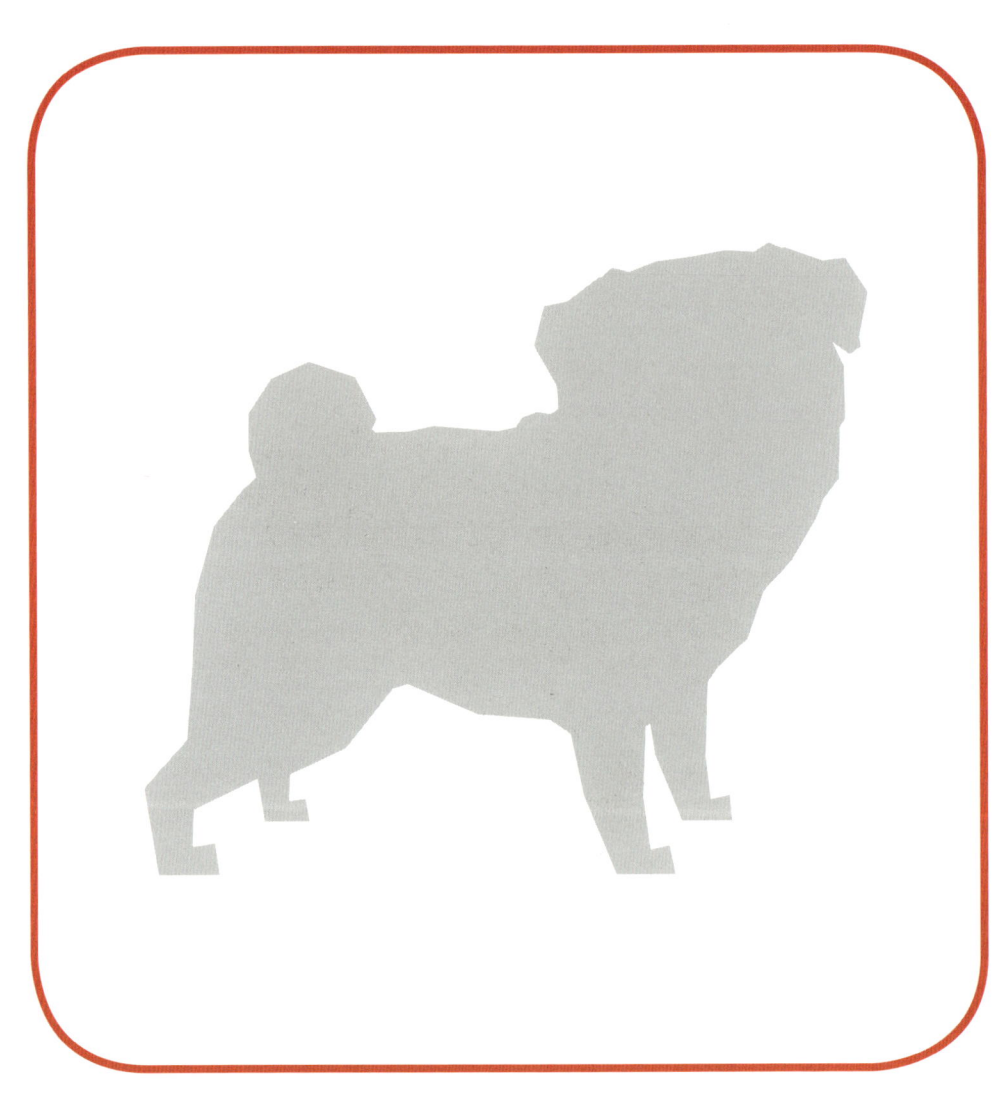

What is it?

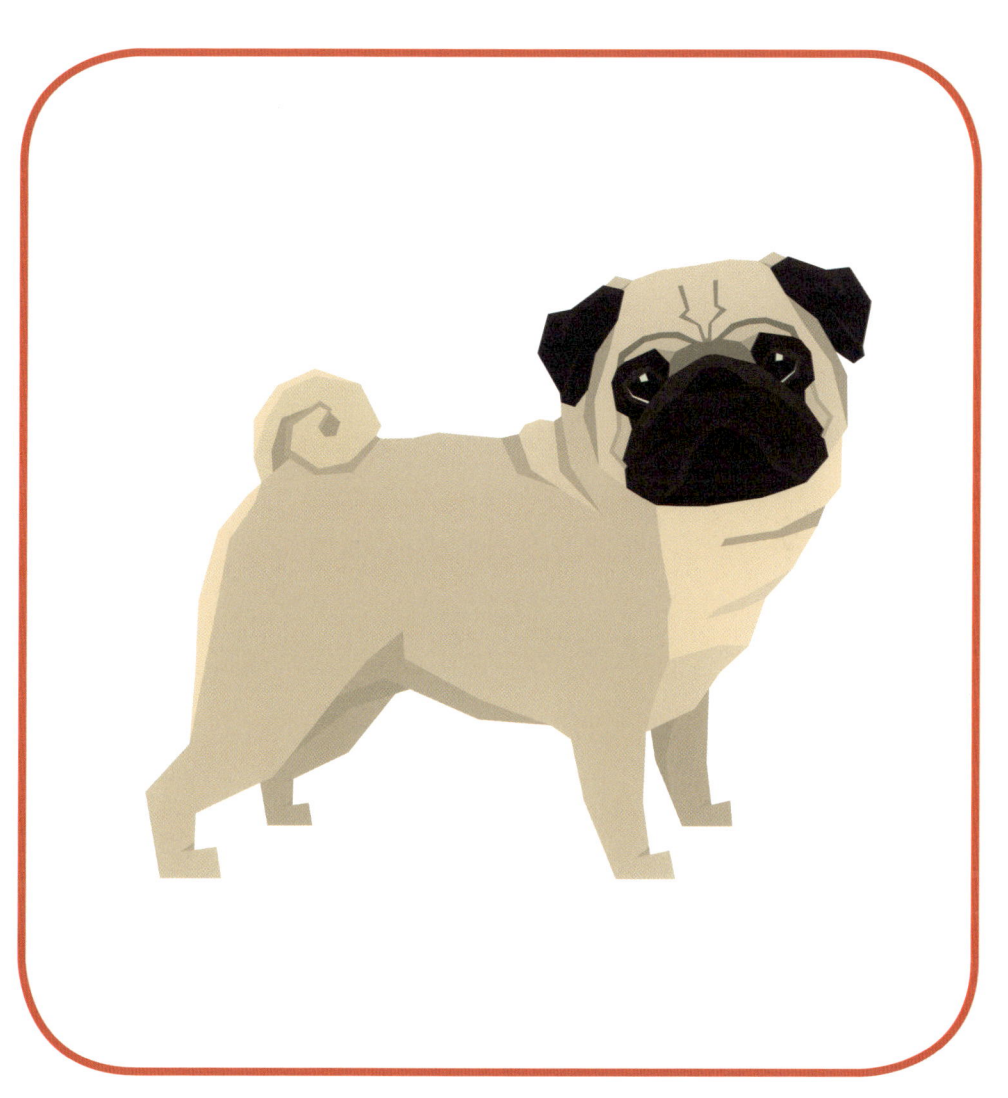

It's a dog.

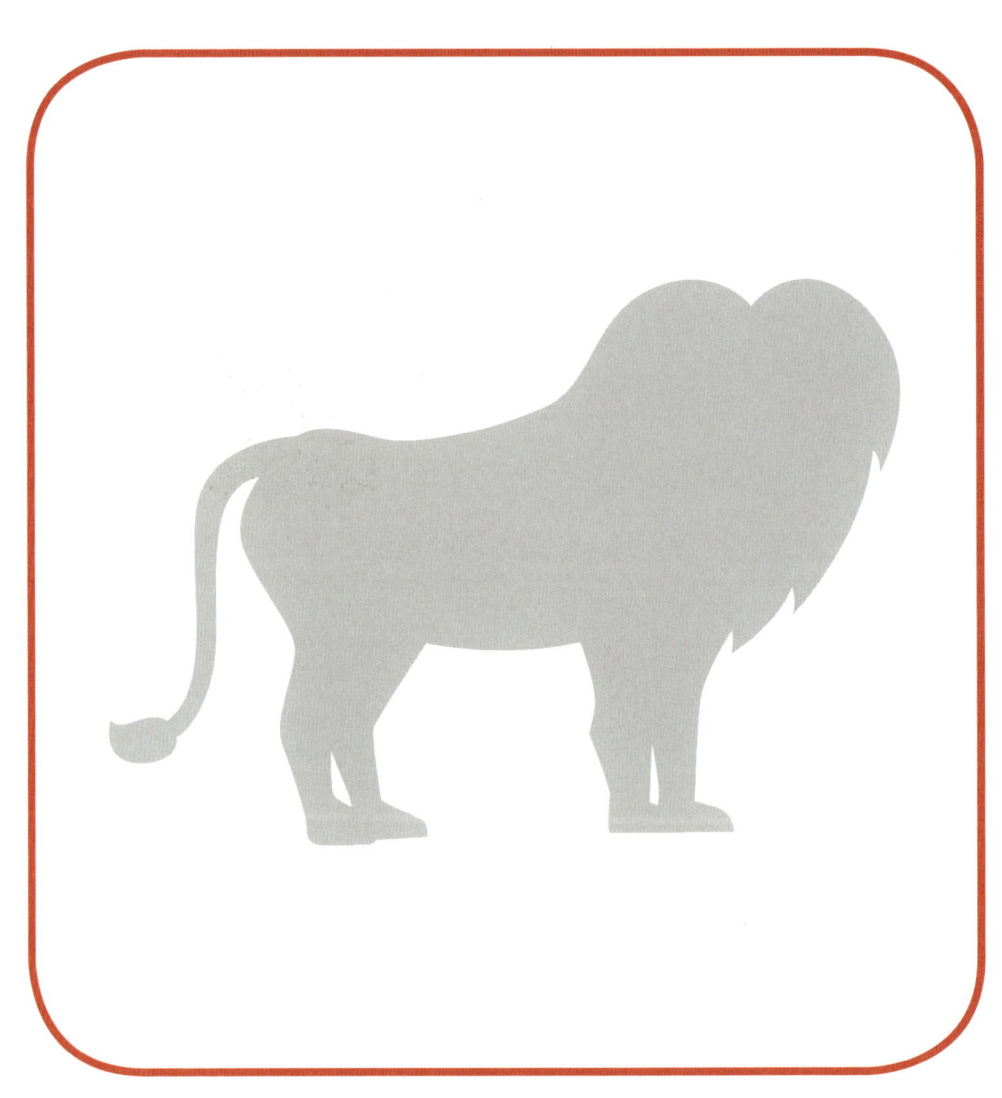

What is it?

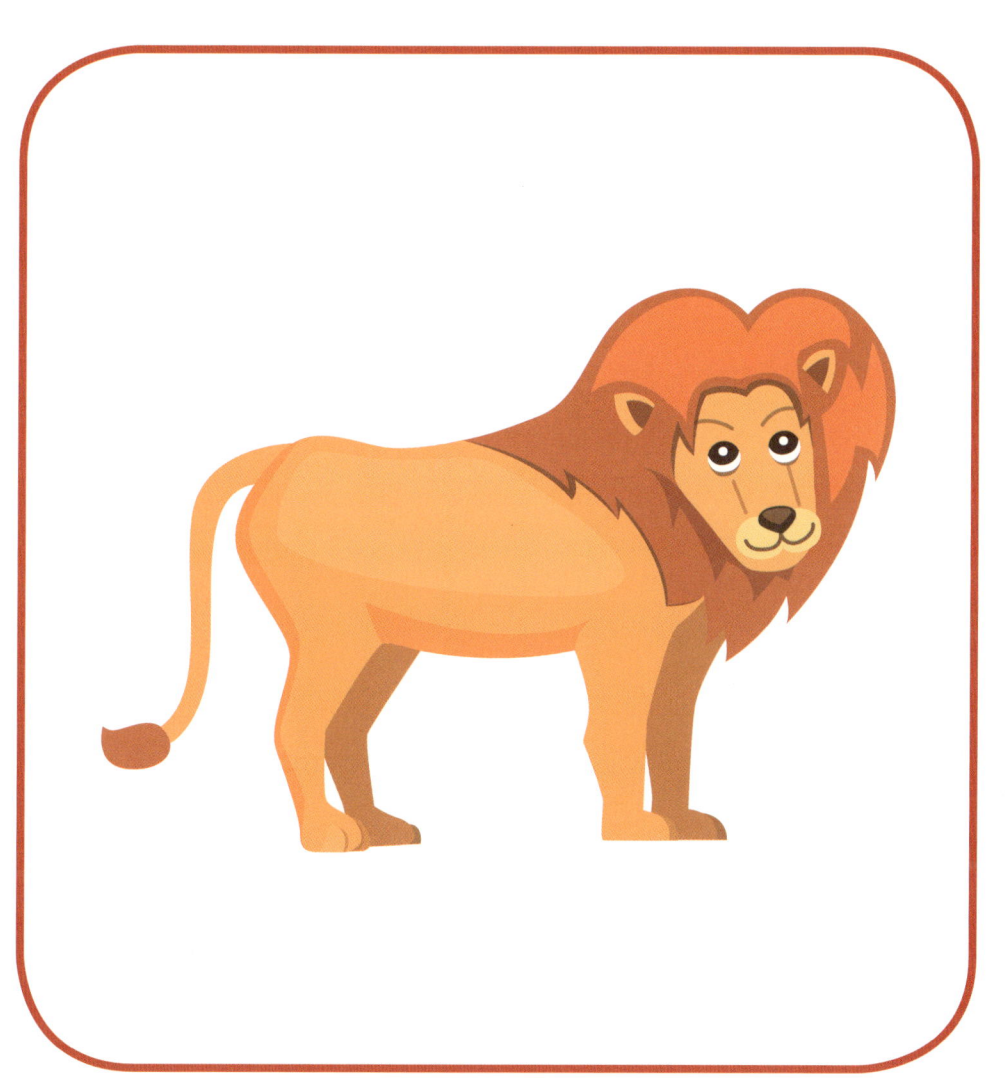

It's a lion.

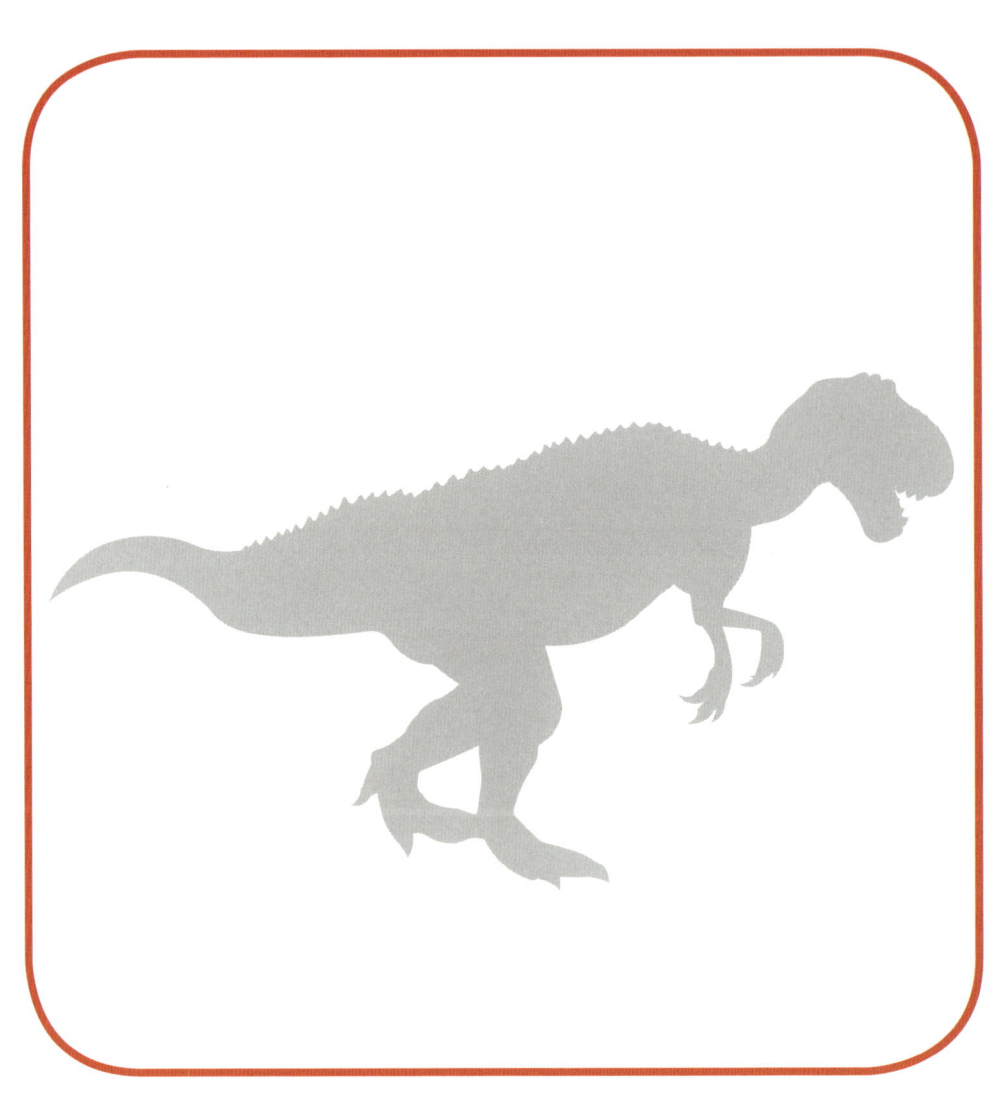

What is it?

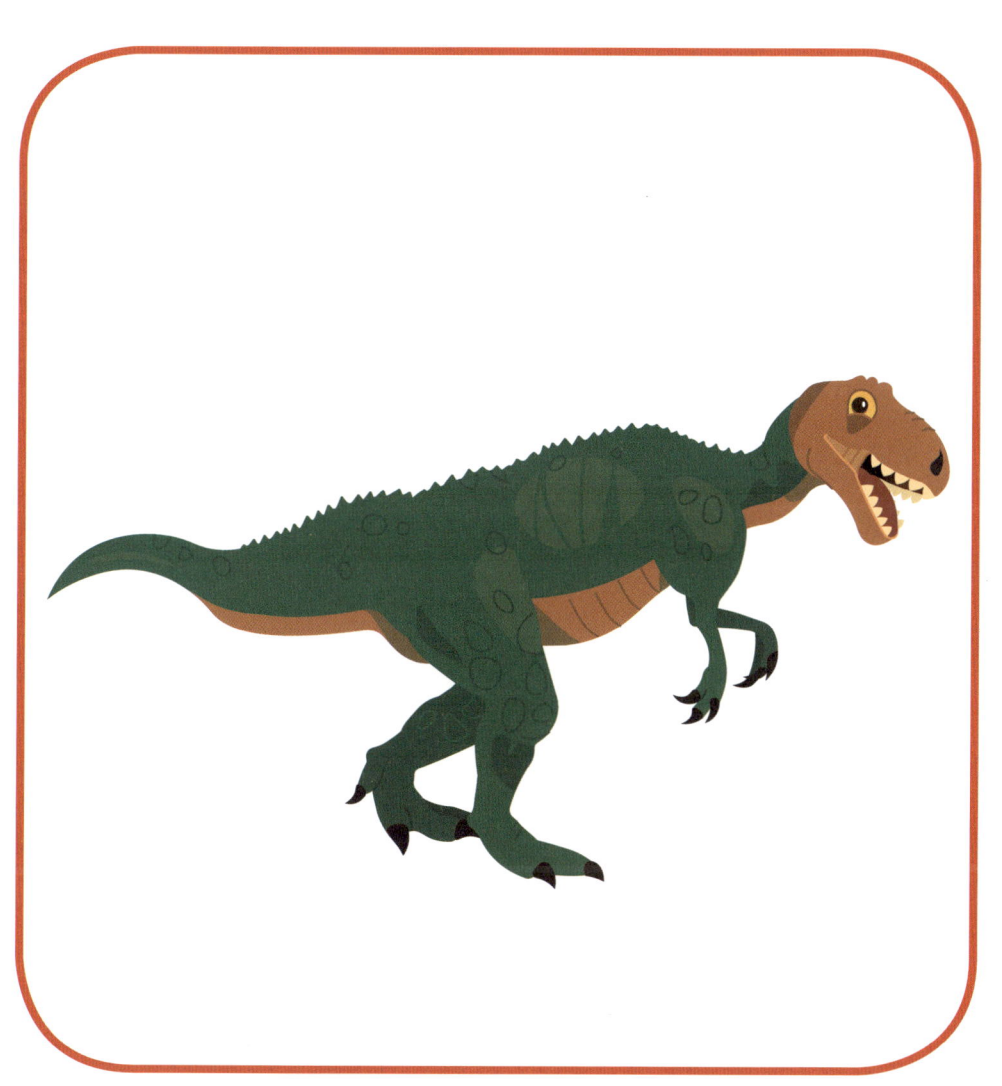

It's a dinosaur.

Let's learn more about the United States of America (USA).

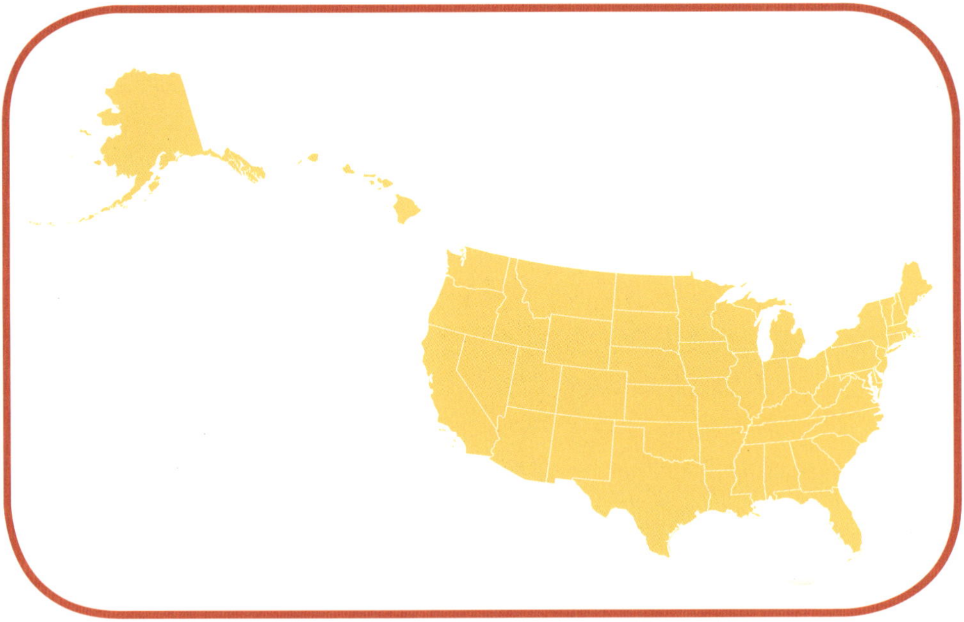

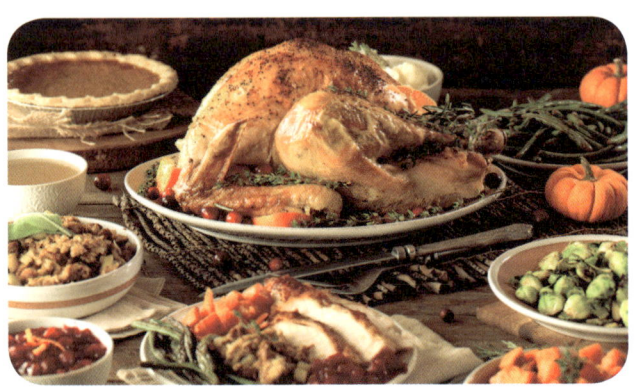

Thanksgiving